Rafael's Gift

by Barbara A. Donovan

ilustrated by Bradley Clark

Harcourt

SCHOOL PUBLISHERS

AF251265

Printed in China

ISBN 10: 0-15-350569-9
ISBN 13: 978-0-15-350569-0

Ordering Options
ISBN 10: 0-15-350336-X (Grade 6 Below-Level Collection)
ISBN 13: 978-0-15-350336-8 (Grade 6 Below-Level Collection)
ISBN 10: 0-15-357574-3 (package of 5)
ISBN 13: 978-0-15-357574-7 (package of 5)

4 5 6 7 8 9 10   0940   12 11 10 09

At the time of this story, a new president was in charge of the Dominican Republic. This president changed the laws. People could no longer speak freely against the government. Newspapers, such as El Caribe, could only print what the government wanted them to print. Germán Ornes believed strongly in a free press. He fought against the rules that restricted what he and others could print.

Streaks of pink, lavender, and orange
shimmered on waters reflecting a dazzling
sunset. In Rafael Garcia's mind, he knew
just how he would paint this sunset if he had
the paper on which to paint it. Lack of paper
tormented Rafael. He'd used up every scrap his
family could spare for his drawings. As a result,
Rafael painted pictures in his mind, hoping for
the day when he'd have enough paper to paint
all his memories.

As the colors darkened in the sky, Rafael realized how late it had become. He grabbed his net bag, which was bursting with the conch he had harvested from the sea floor, and raced along the meandering path to his home.

Mami was cutting tomatoes and onions for the conch stew when Rafael arrived home. "Your father is out at the bench waiting for you," Mami called as Rafael appeared at the screen door. "Go help him clean the conch. There's a surprise for you out there, too," she said with a warm smile.

Rafael headed out back to where he could
see his father and another man sitting in the
shade. As Rafael surveyed the scene, he began
to grin. "Tio Germán!" he called excitedly to his
father's best friend.

Rafael loved this family friend whom he
called his uncle. He was proud of the way he
led the fight for free speech in their country.
That Tío Germán was visiting his father was a
rare delight for the entire family. Rafael emptied
the conch onto the bench and began working
with his father to separate the sweet juicy
conch meat from its hard shell.

Tio Germán questioned Rafael about school
and about his baseball team. Then he inquired,
"Do you know I still have that painting you
made for me? It's hanging on the wall of my
office. It helps me remember the beauty and
innocence of my island home."

Rafael blushed with pride. He had painted a
scene of a boy on a beach with his arms spread
wide open as if to hug the world. He had given
it to Tio Germán for his birthday last year.
He did not know that his father's friend had
actually hung it in his office. "What have you
painted recently, Rafael?" Tio Germán asked.

8

Rafael gazed down at his lap and replied, "Nothing lately, Tio Germán."

"Do you not like to paint anymore?" asked Tio Germán with concern in his voice.

"Oh, yes, Tio Germán," Rafael hurriedly reassured him, "but I do not have any paper."

Tio Germán leaned back in his chair and smiled. "Then you might just want to take a look in the backseat of my car when you bring this conch back up to your mother. There's a present for you in a brown box."

Rafael beamed as he thanked Tio Germán for the gift he had yet to see. Then he scooped all the conch meat into a bowl and excused himself. Mami barely had time to thank him for such quick work before Rafael was out the door, headed for Tio Germán's car.

One time, Tio Germán had brought Rafael an end roll of paper from his workplace at *El Caribe*. As the newspaper was printed, the workers would change the rolls of paper before they reached the end of the roll. Tio Germán had thought that Rafael might want to use the paper that his pressmen would throw out. Was it possible that Tio Germán had brought Rafael another roll of paper this time?

When Rafael reached the black car sitting in the shade of the gri gri tree, he peeked into the back window where he saw a large carton. Rafael leaned into the backseat. His hand hovered over the carton. What if this were not paper after all?

Eventually, Rafael maneuvered the carton from the car. When he slit open the top, he stumbled back because inside were not one, but five end rolls of paper! Rafael had never had so much paper in his life. The many images he'd saved in his mind jostled for attention. He didn't know which one to draw first.

With a grunt, Rafael heaved the carton up into his arms and ran into his room. He cut off one piece of paper and laid it tenderly on his table. Looking out the window, he could see his father and Tio Germán still talking outside. Rafael remembered stories his father had told him of the fun he and his friend had had in their youth.

Making light strokes with his pencil, Rafael's fingers fairly danced across the paper. Subtle lines joined as forms took shape on the page. Soon, two figures emerged among the swirling lines. From a box under his bed, Rafael chose the colors he'd use to bring his sketch to life. By the time Mami's conch stew was ready, Rafael's gift for Tio Germán was ready, too.

After stuffing themselves on stew, Mami, Papi, and Tio Germán brought their coffee out onto the porch where they listened to *merengue* music on the radio. Rafael went to his room to get his drawing. Returning to the porch, he handed the completed drawing to his uncle. In it, two boys resembling Papi and Tio Germán frolicked in the surf as if they had not a care in the world. In one corner he had written, "To Tio Germán, with thanks for all you have done and will do for all of us. Rafael Garcia."

Tio Germán wiped a tear that leaked from his eye. Then he nodded his thanks to the boy who could touch his heart and help him remember the best of times during the worst of times.

Think Critically

1. What kind of paper did Tio Germán give to Rafael?

2. If you could be any character in this story, which character would you be? Explain why.

3. To Tio Germán, why was his youth the best of times and the present the worst of times?

4. In what way(s) is Rafael like a character from another story that you've read?

5. Why do you think Rafael painted the picture of his father and Tio Germán as boys at the beach instead of the sunset he had just seen?

 **Language Arts**

Write a Thank You Note Write a thank you note from Tio Germán to Rafael to express how much the painting means to him.

School-Home Connection Discuss with your family how your lives would change if there was little or no paper to write or draw on.

Word Count: 947